IT'S TIME TO EAT GERMAN CHICKEN

It's Time to Eat GERMAN CHICKEN

Walter the Educator

Silent King Books
A WhichHead Entertainment Imprint

Copyright © 2025 by Walter the Educator

All rights reserved. No part of this book may be reproduced in any manner whatsoever without written per- mission except in the case of brief quotations embodied in critical articles and reviews.

First Printing, 2024

Disclaimer

This book is a literary work; the story is not about specific persons, locations, situations, and/or circumstances unless mentioned in a historical context. Any resemblance to real persons, locations, situations, and/or circumstances is coincidental. This book is for entertainment and informational purposes only. The author and publisher offer this information without warranties expressed or implied. No matter the grounds, neither the author nor the publisher will be accountable for any losses, injuries, or other damages caused by the reader's use of this book. The use of this book acknowledges an understanding and acceptance of this disclaimer.

It's Time to Eat GERMAN CHICKEN is a collectible early learning book by Walter the Educator suitable for all ages belonging to Walter the Educator's Time to Eat Book Series. Collect more books at WaltertheEducator.com

USE THE EXTRA SPACE TO TAKE NOTES AND DOCUMENT YOUR MEMORIES

GERMAN CHICKEN

It's time to eat, hooray hooray,

It's Time to Eat

German Chicken

German Chicken's on the way!

Golden brown and crispy too,

A yummy meal for me and you.

With spices warm and herbs so sweet,

It smells so good, we tap our feet!

The table's set, the napkins shine,

Time to eat, it's chicken time!

First a drumstick, juicy fun,

German Chicken's number one!

Dip it in some mustard bright,

Every bite feels just so right.

Potatoes dance beside the plate,

Cabbage twirls, we just can't wait!

German flavors, bold and fine,

We sit down and start to dine.

It's Time to Eat

German Chicken

Crunchy outside, soft inside,

This chicken's such a tasty ride.

We use our forks and napkins too,

Minding manners, yes, we do!

"Pass the sauce!" my sister cheers,

German Chicken disappears!

Big bites here and little there,

Chicken magic everywhere.

We take a sip of apple juice,

It helps the flavors turn so loose.

Yum and yum, oh what a treat,

German Chicken can't be beat!

The table hums with happy sounds,

Forks and spoons go round and round.

Every bite, a tasty spark,

It's Time to Eat

German Chicken

Like fireworks dancing in the dark.

Soon the plate is shining clear,

German Chicken disappears!

We clap our hands and say "Thank you!"

For a meal so warm and true.

Bellies full and smiles wide,

Happy feelings bloom inside.

German Chicken saved the day,

It's Time to Eat

German Chicken

Let's eat it every meal, hooray!

ABOUT THE CREATOR

Walter the Educator is one of the pseudonyms for Walter Anderson. Formally educated in Chemistry, Business, and Education, he is an educator, an author, a diverse entrepreneur, and he is the son of a disabled war veteran. "Walter the Educator" shares his time between educating and creating. He holds interests and owns several creative projects that entertain, enlighten, enhance, and educate, hoping to inspire and motivate you. Follow, find new works, and stay up to date with Walter the Educator™ at WaltertheEducator.com

www.ingramcontent.com/pod-product-compliance
Lightning Source LLC
LaVergne TN
LVHW052012060526
838201LV00059B/3988